As You Step Out Today

A 30 day daily reminder of God's word to you

VOLUME 4

BUSOLA ADUN

AS YOU STEP OUT TODAY (Volume 1)

Copyright © Busola Adun 2020
ISBN: 978-1-8381837-0-7

Published by:
Grace House Publishing Company
www.gracehousepublishing.org

Unless otherwise indicated, all Scripture quotations are taken from the Amplfied Version (AMP) of the Bible.

All rights reserved.
No portion of this book may be used
without the written permission of the
publisher, with the exception of brief
excerpts in magazines, articles, reviews, etc.

DEVOTIONAL TESTIMONIALS

Bzioninspires daily devotional blog is a free gift that blesses and encourages so many people. The author, Busola Joan Adun, taps into the Holy Spirit and writes exactly what you need to hear to be guided and strengthened for the day. The blog often seems as though it is written to you specifically. That personal connection is also made as she starts each blog saying, "As you step out today..." or "My prayer for you today is...". Since this blog is written for YOU, I encourage you to take a few minutes to read it and benefit from the anointing and words of wisdom they contain. You'll be glad you did!

Prophetess Cynthia Murray
Founder Divine Women of Destiny Ministries International

Here's a Reminder of God's Word to You...! I've not been a fan of daily devotionals because I perceived I needed not to waste my time reading writers' expressions of their personal encounters/insights, which could be peculiar to their unique circumstances or situations. However, your style of presentation is so exceptional, in that you don't impose on me your thoughts; you don't make it feel like there's something new you're bringing my way, rather you stir up in me vital dormant knowledge in the order of Peter (2 Peter 1:12). "Here's a Reminder... "You will always say, yet they come as fresh as the morning dew. More Grace, Joan!

Alex Ogoke

From the moment I started reading the daily devotionals, they really impacted my day, my thoughts, my behaviour, and my attitude towards others and myself. The daily devotionals imparted a desire within me to live out the Word of God in my life. It was while reading one of the devotionals that I came to understand that God is responsible for me, and this revolutionized my thinking. I believe it was at that point that I truly grasped the depths of God's love for me and how He sees me and helped me to accept, without doubt, such great love. The daily devotionals always come through at a time when I need them most. Therefore, I know that the servant whom God has used to pen these devotionals has been called by God to draw His children closer to Him and be a light to those who are still searching. I look forward to receiving the daily devotionals, as they are worded with such simplicity yet are powerful, and I know they are moulding me into God's likeness. Thank you for allowing God to use you in such a wonderful and effective way.

Samantha Weekes

The morning devotion by Pastor Busola Joan Adun has been a tremendous blessing. It is always a joy and a blessing when you are in your room at night meditating on a word, and in the morning, you get one of the daily devotionals talking about precisely what one was meditating about the night before. It is very encouraging, and you can almost feel the heart of the writer. It's amazing the day Pastor Adun wrote up her devotion one day at our house. I was amazed! There was no copy and pasting! She typed every single letter herself! (And the Holy Spirit inspiring her, of course). I say God bless you, and the oil upon your head will always be fresh. You're a blessing to this generation!

Foluso Olatunji

These daily devotionals are truly Holy Spirit inspired. They offer great encouragement and have often aligned with my daily meditation in the Word. They have truly blessed me, and I am pleased that Pastor Busola is finally making them available for all.

Donna Griffith-Sackey,
Co-author of Tame Your Boss

ABOUT THE DEVOTIONAL

▼

"This Book of the Law shall not depart from your mouth, but you shall read [and meditate on] it day and night, so that you may be careful to do [everything] in accordance with all that is written in it; for then you will make your way prosperous, and then you will be successful." Joshua 1:8 [AMP]

As you step out today, the first in the five volumes series is a practical daily devotional put together to help set your day's direction and influence your thoughts and actions as you go about your daily business and activities. It comprises a compilation of faith-building devotional write-ups inspired by the Holyspirit to influence your thoughts, attitudes, and behaviours in alignment with your kingdom identity. Each devotional consists of daily reminders based on scriptural references from the Bible to encourage and empower you as a believer to live out God's word in your daily activities intentionally. Especially in your interaction with colleagues, business partners, clients, friends, and families and those who are not of the Christian faith. This devotional also challenges you as a child of God to live worthy of your call as a royal priesthood and Christ ambassador (1 Peter 2:9). To arise and shine your light and continually be a blessing and a giver of hope to others as you carry out your daily business and activities.

DEDICATION
▼

"The Lord GOD has given me the tongue of those who are instructed to know how to sustain the weary with a word. He awakens me each morning; He awakens my ear to listen like those being instructed". Isaiah 50:4 [TLB]

This devotional is dedicated to the Holyspirit, the supreme intelligence who inspires me with his words of wisdom, gives me divine insight and instructs me to write faith-filled words that encourage others in their daily Christian walk. I am grateful to the Holyspirit for how 'He awakens My ear' to pen down words of hope that lifts others' faith and how He gently nudges me to weave my personal experiences and challenges. In a way that has offered encouragement to several people, while many have also found strength and hope to keep trusting God. As they are reminded through His word that He is a good and faithful God who keeps his word and is no respecter of persons.

DAY 01

HE KNOWS YOUR NAME

As you step out today, here's a reminder of God's word to you from Isaiah 43:1 [AMP & NIV].

> *"But now, this is what the Lord says— he who created you, Jacob, he who formed you, Israel: "Do not fear, for I have redeemed you; [from captivity]; I have called [summoned] you by name; you are Mine."*

Today's Bible verse reminds us as believers of how valuable we are to God. It is a loving reminder of God's personal and individual care for you and me as his children. Think for a few seconds of what God's daily schedule must be and look like with the close to 8 billion people on earth. Yet, despite the size and magnitude of the world's population, God knows each of us by name and calls us his own. When we read and study the Bible we see that God is a relational God. A God that longs to relate to us on a one on one basis because he cares for us and loves us recklessly.

So, despite God being the creator of the universe and the designer of mankind, He never gets our names mixed up! (What an awesome attribute that is about our great God. He doesn't get confused with our names, neither does he forgets our name. He is so particular about every detail of our lives that He has also inscribed our names in the palm of his hands.

Isaiah 49:16 [NLT]

> *"See, I have written (inscribed, engraved) your name on the palms of my hands.*

And he is aware of every hair on our head – (Luke 12:7, Matthew 10:30).

> *"And the very hairs on your head are all numbered. So don't be afraid; you are more valuable to God than a whole flock of sparrows."*

Despite the awesomeness and greatness of God and all that our God get busy doing, yet He is never too busy for us when we call out to him because he calls us his own.

I reckon you have been in situations where you recently saw someone you knew some years ago but you no longer remember their name. Or perhaps you met someone recently but few minutes of meeting that person, you completely forgot their name. Or it could be the reverse where you met an acquaintance who just couldn't remember your name. If you are like me, I end up feeling bad whenever that happens. Situations like this only shows or reflects the frailty of mankind.

But how comforting to know that God is not like us, He never forgets our name, he never forgets the name of the one he created and formed in his image… let me emphasize this truth by saying that it's is impossible for God to forget your name or my name. It's just one of the things that God can never do. He says "you are mine" you are his beloved and because you are his beloved, he lovingly calls you by name. The Psalmist understood this love relationship between God and his beloved children that he beautifully captures it in these words.

Psalm 139:17 *"**How precious it is, Lord, to realize that you are thinking about me constantly! I can't even count how many times a day your thoughts turn toward me. And when I waken in the morning, you are still thinking of me!**"* David, knew without any shadow of doubt that God knew his name hence why he would think about him all day.

So, no matter how emotionally low you might be feeling right now due to certain situations or circumstances you might be going through. Never entertain the thought that God has forgotten you because He can't and He never will because he has your name constantly before him, he calls you by name and says you are his own.

Therefore, as you go about your daily business and activities today, I encourage you to meditate on this truth from today's Bible verse and rejoice knowing that out of the 7.7 billion people on earth. God remembers your name, calls you his own and for this reason, I trust that he will show you his favour and pour out his blessings continually upon you and all that concerns you in Jesus name.

Do have a blessed and productive day!

DAY 02

LIFE IN CHRIST

As you step out today, here's a reminder of God's word to you from Ephesians 4:23-31 [TLB, NLT, AMP].

²³ "Now your attitudes and thoughts must all be constantly changing for the better [Let the Spirit renew your thoughts and attitudes]. ²⁴ Yes, you must be a new and different person [put on the new self [the regenerated and renewed nature], created in God's image, [godlike] in the righteousness and holiness of the truth [living in a way that expresses to God your gratitude for your salvation].

²⁵ Stop lying to each other [whether defrauding, telling half-truths, spreading rumors, any such as these]; tell the truth, for we are parts of each other and when we lie to each other we are hurting ourselves. ²⁶ If you are angry, don't sin by nursing your grudge. Don't let the sun go down with you still angry—get over it quickly;

²⁷ for when you are angry, you give a mighty foothold to the devil. [And do not give the devil an opportunity to lead you into sin by holding a grudge, or nurturing anger, or harboring resentment, or cultivating bitterness].

²⁸ If anyone is stealing he must stop it and begin using those hands of his for honest work so he can give to others in need.

²⁹ Don't use bad language [Do not let unwholesome [foul, profane, worthless, vulgar] words ever come out of your mouth]. Say only what is good and helpful to those you are talking to, and what will give them a blessing [but only such speech as is good for building up others, according to the need and the occasion, so that it will be a blessing to those who hear [you speak].

³⁰ Don't cause the Holy Spirit sorrow by the way you live [And do not grieve the Holy Spirit of God [but seek to please Him]. Remember, he is the one who marks you to be present on that day when salvation from sin will be complete [by whom you were sealed and marked [branded as God's own] for the day of redemption [the final deliverance from the consequences of sin].

³¹ Stop being mean, bad-tempered, and angry. Quarrelling, harsh words, and dislike of others should have no place in your lives [Let all bitterness and wrath and anger and clamor [perpetual animosity, resentment, strife, fault-finding] and slander be put away from you, along with every kind of malice [all spitefulness, verbal abuse, malevolence]. ³² Instead, be kind and helpful to each other, tenderhearted [compassionate, understanding], forgiving one another [readily and freely], just as God has forgiven you because you belong to Christ.

Today's key verses in a nutshell are a reminder of how our lives in Christ as believers must look and reflect to others. It carefully outlines to us as believers God's expectations of us as it relates to our spiritual growth. And how the spiritual change we daily experience through the Holyspirit is required to impact on our everyday attitudes, character, thoughts and behaviour.

Today's Bible verses furthermore speaks so powerfully and clearly to us as believers especially as regarding our lifestyle as believers. Our relationship and disposition with others especially people who are not of the faith. And most importantly how we should ensure that we do not grieve or bring sorrow to God's Holyspirit (the seal for our redemption) by the way we live.

Apostle Paul in this heartfelt letter to the Ephesians church, a letter which still speaks powerfully to us Christians living in the 21st century today, reminds believers to live worthy of the call to which we have been called. And to be the light (i.e. an embodiment of the spirit of God) in the darkness that reflects the multidimensional love of God.

Therefore, as you go about your daily business and activities today, I encourage you to turn today's Bible verses into prayer points for yourself and make declarations where necessary, for instance you can declare these words:

> *"I am renewed in the spirit of my mind and I put on the new person which was created by God in true righteousness and holiness. I will not grieve or bring sorrow to the Holyspirit but honor him in both in my words, in my actions and in the way I live. Only wholesome words that brings blessings will proceed from my mouth to others in Jesus name,"*

Also, carefully meditate on today's Bible passage to examine yourself to see where you may have fallen short.

And where you have fallen short, sincerely ask God (your Heavenly Father) for his forgiveness in line with his word in 1John 1:8-9 ***"If we say we have no sin, we deceive ourselves, and the truth is not in us. But if we confess our sins to him, he is faithful and just to forgive us our sins and to cleanse us from all wickedness and unrighteousness."***

Be sure to continually seek the help of the Holyspirit in your everyday Christian life (making sure that the Holyspirit is never grieved by your words and actions) especially as it relates with your interaction with both believers and unbelievers.

Remember, God wants us to live an honourable, exemplary and selfless life that sets us distinctively apart from those who are unsaved. A life that will attract many others to us, to our kingdom lifestyle and cause people to (ask us what makes us different) want to know our God and to glorify him.

Do have a blessed and productive day!

DAY 03

BE A CHRIST INFLUENCER

As you step out today, here's a reminder of God's word to you from 1 Timothy 4:12 [NLT].

> *"Don't let anyone think less of you because you are young. Be an example to all believers in what you say, in the way you live, in your love, your faith, and your purity."*

The MSG Translation says,

> *"Get the word out. Teach all these things. And don't let anyone put you down because you're young. Teach believers with your life: by word, by demeanor, by love, by faith, by integrity."*

Today's Bible verse in a nutshell I believe can also be summed up in this statement – be an influencer for Christ. This is because to be an example to others (whether believers or unbelievers) [in what you say, in the way you live, in your love, your faith, and your purity] is also to have the capacity to influence others. To influence means to have the capacity to effect change in a person's character, behavior or attitude.

To be a Christ influencer therefore, requires you to first, see yourself as someone who carries precious treasures (2 Corinthians 4:7) that is constantly looking for opportunities to offer that treasure to others too.

Apostle Paul wanted Timothy to understand the influence he could command simply by living a life of integrity influenced by the Holyspirit. The power and importance of influence was further reiterated as I watched a scene from my favorite TV soapie where just by a social media influencer posing with a copy of an entertainment magazine and posting the picture with the hashtag of the magazine on their social media page. The level of online views and readership for the newspaper company skyrocketed tremendously. Thereby attracting more potential advertisers and increasing their profit.

This singular act made the company CEO engage (i.e. offer them a contract) the influencer as their brand ambassador. Why? Simply because of the power of influence this individual had on their followers to influence their behaviour.

2 Corinthians 5:20 reminds us that *"we are ambassadors for Christ, i.e. Christ's representatives ..."* so as Christ representatives we are called to influence others positively such that our exemplary lifestyle will compel them to want to know Christ and also be a Christ follower.

So what does it mean to be a Christ influencer? This simply means living a Holyspirit centric life that transforms you inside out – [i.e. it transforms your character, behaviour and lifestyle] and the people who come in contact with you are influenced by your lifestyle that they want to imitate you too.

In a world where social media has garnered so much power and influence, it is becoming needful for many believers to arise from the shadows, to take their place and to have a voice that brings about influence.

For example, take a quick tour on a social media such as IG, and you will be amazed at how many known companies engage opinion leaders (individuals or celebrities) with huge followership that can influence their followers to buy into their ideals, goods or services. These opinion leaders have so much influence that they could also lure people in making wrong and poor choices.

Unfortunately, there are many ungodly influencers who permeate the social space and through their power of influence, they have influenced many people negatively and in other instances led even believers astray.

This is why as believers we must arise and be intentional about being a Christ influencer:

- ❖ One who points others to Christ
- ❖ One who speaks life and hope to others,
- ❖ One who live life by example in what they in love, in faith, in purity, in what they say and in how they live their lives

Therefore, as you go about your daily business and activities today, I encourage you to be a Christ influencer in your workplace, college, university, on the bus, in the train, in the aeroplane, at the train station, your children school, social media platform etc.

Take advantage of opportunities that allow you to influence others positively. Also, make use of every opportunity social media platform affords to shine the light of Christ to your followers and those who you come in contact with on your social media page.

Be intentional about what you post and how you comment on

others page so that through you words, deeds and lifestyle, it influence others to want to be a better person. And remember, just like Apostle Paul admonished Timothy, it is important to never let anyone intimidate or make you feel you don't have the power to influence others because of your age or status. You are called by Christ to be the salt and light (Matthew 5:13-16) of the world and that's the order you need to fulfill your mandate as a Christ influencer! (Mark 16:15 & Matthew 28:19-20).

Choose to be an influencer for Christ every day.

Do have a blessed and productive day!

DAY 04

IT'S GOD'S BREATHE IN YOUR LUNGS

As you step out today here's a reminder of God's word to you from Psalm 150:6 [TLB].

"Let everything alive give praises to the Lord! You praise him!"

The [AMP] Translation says,

"Let everything that has breath and every breath of life praise the Lord! Praise the Lord! (Hallelujah!)"

The [NIV] Translation says,

"Let everything that has breath praise the LORD (sing praises to the Lord) Praise the LORD!

The [MSG] Translation says,

"Let every living, breathing creature praise God! Hallelujah!"

As I think and meditate on today's key scripture, the lyrics of the powerful song 'Great are you Lord' by Michael W Smith floods my mind.

" It's your breath in our lungs
So we pour out our praise

We pour out our praise
It's Your breath in our lungs
So we pour out our praise to You only.
And all the earth will shout your praise.
Our hearts will cry, these bones will sing
Great are You, Lord."

We are alive this beautiful morning because of the breath that the Lord has poured out into our lungs. Pause and think for a moment – what if your lungs had been deprived of air (oxygen) while you slept? However if that is not your case and you are reading this devotional right now then that tells me you meet the criteria of today's key verse – Let everything that has breathe praise the Lord and today is yet another opportunity to live out this scripture – **Let everything, let every living thing that has breath, Praise the Lord**. Wow, what an awesome gift we have been given by our Heavenly Father!

And while you are praising the Lord, I encourage you to let your heart be filled with gratitude as you intentionally thank God for the many blessings and benefits, he bestows on you, your family and loved ones daily.

So, I ask you this morning again is there breath in you?

Has God forgiven you of your sins?

Has God showed you His mercies?

Has God been an ever-present help in times of need?

Has God taken away your shame and given you hope?

Has God ever made a way where there seemed to be no way?

Has God made situations that seemed impossible, possible for you?

Has God ever stepped into any challenging situation that you found yourself in?

Has God ever met your financial needs and made provisions for you just when you need it?

Has God ever answered your prayers and turned around your captivity that you almost imagined you were dreaming?

Then, make out time out of your busy schedule today just to say Thank you, ABBA Father and let your exorbitant worship and praises pour to Him just like David poured it out to God (2 Samuel 6:14)

Therefore, as you go about your daily business and activities today, be intentional about praising God even if your circumstances do not look like the one you want to praise or thank Him about. Take your time to give God praise for His tender mercies, goodness, and faithfulness in your life and family!

Our Heavenly Father is a faithful, loving, good, kind, merciful and mighty God whose love towards us is everlasting. His love chases after us even in our weakness and shortfalls. He never leaves us or forsakes us and He always fulfils his promises to us because it is not in his nature to lie, change His mind or fail to bring His promises to pass in our lives no matter how long it may seem.

He is our perfect God that provides us with strength daily to accomplish our task (think about it, if God doesn't provide you with strength for each day to carry out your duties, what can you do?) and He has poured his breathe to see the dawn of each new day.

So, if you are truly appreciative of all that your loving Heavenly Father has done for you and your family through the years, then let his praises fill your mouth today and always.

Saturate your environment with songs of worship and praise unto your Heavenly Father whether you are at home, in the car, train, bus, taking a walk or even at your workplace (you can do this during your break time). Intentionally, create an atmosphere that will usher in God's presence and before you know it your spirit becomes overwhelmed with God's presence and your heart is filled with His peace.

Remember, God is enthroned in the praises of His people so lift up your praises to Him for He is good, and His faithfulness endures forever and throughout all generations, Hallelujah!

Do have a blessed and productive day!

DAY 05

A PRAYER OF THANKSGIVING UNTO THE LORD

As you step out today here's a reminder of God's word to you from Psalm 138:1-8 [MSG].

1-3 Thank you! Everything in me says "Thank you!"
  Angels listen as I sing my thanks.
I kneel in worship facing your holy temple
  and say it again: "Thank you!"
Thank you for your love,
  thank you for your faithfulness;
Most holy is your name,
  most holy is your Word.
The moment I called out, you stepped in;
  you made my life large with strength.

4-6 When they hear what you have to say, God,
  all earth's kings will say "Thank you."
They'll sing of what you've done:
  "How great the glory of God!"
And here's why: God, high above, sees far below;
  no matter the distance, he knows everything about us.

7-8 When I walk into the thick of trouble,
  keep me alive in the angry turmoil.

With one hand
  strike my foes,
With your other hand
  save me.
Finish what you started in me, God.
  Your love is eternal—don't quit on me now.

This is the day the Lord has made, let us rejoice and be glad it. What a blessing to see the break of a new day. A day filed with an abundance and overflow of God's blessings because the Bible tells us in Psalm 68:19 **"Blessed be the Lord, Who daily loads us with benefits, The God of our salvation!"**

It is a new day to thank God for his goodness, faithfulness and mercies over our lives and families.

Therefore, as you go about your daily business and activities, take time to meditate on this Bible passage and let a prayer of thanksgiving break forth from your heart to your mouth and to your heavenly Father for his love and constant care towards you, your family, friends and loved ones,

I pray that you will experience the help and the favour of the Lord in all of your endeavours this day, this week and in this month in Jesus name.

Do have a blessed and productive day!

DAY 06

TAKE ADVANTAGE OF EVERY OPPORTUNITY

As you step out today, here's a reminder of God's word to you from Ephesians 5:16-17 [NIV].

"…making the most of every opportunity (making the best use of time), because the days are evil. Therefore, do not be foolish, but understand what the Lord's will is."

The [NLT] Translation says,

"Make the most of every opportunity in these evil days. Don't act thoughtlessly but understand what the Lord wants you to do."

In the book of 2 Timothy 3:16, the Bible states that all scripture is useful to teach us what is true and to instruct us. Today's key verse is one of such scriptures that is instructing us as believers on how to live, how to understand what God's will is and how to make the most of every opportunity in these evil days we live in.

Today's Bible verse says it loud and clear that we live in 'evil days' hence why we have to be very intentional about making use and taking advantage of every opportunity that we have to be a blessing to others wherever we find ourselves and especially to share the good news of Christ to others.

Opportunities can present itself to us in terms of time, business, relationships, education etc. People all around us are going through so many hard times that they need encouragement and wouldn't mind someone to pray for them. As believers, God wants us to step out into each 'new day' and be sensitive to his spirit to know what he wants us to do and how to take advantage of the opportunities he brings our way.

I recall many times starting my day with my well laid out plan on all I need to accomplish or get done for the day. However, God interrupts my plans because he presents to me an opportunity or opportunities to encourage someone who needs someone to talk to as they go through certain challenges. Life is short, so it is imperative to daily pursue everything that God has called you to do and do everything within your power to kill **Procrastination**.

Therefore, as you go about your daily business and activities today, make use of every opportunity that God presents to you whether at work, on the train, bus, plane etc. The opportunities might be to encourage someone with your testimony, share a word of prayer, show them how to do a task etc. Make sure you don't let your weaknesses or what you seemingly think you don't have stop and rob you of being a blessing to others or stop you from stepping out with the ideas that God has put inside of you to be a blessing to your community and nations of the world.

So, step out today and use your talents, gifts, and ideas to create products, business or ministry that will be a solution to some of the problems in the community/ nation. Live each day with these focus in mind – to be a blessing to others and to live each day fulfilling God's purpose for your life! Live each day determined to live out God's purpose for your life without any apology to anyone.

Remember, everyone God used in the bible to accomplish great things in their communities and nations seemed unqualified to the people around them, yet God carried out His agenda through each and every one of them. No doubt, God uses the foolish things of this world to confound the wise! (1Corinthians 1:27). ***BE WISE AND TAKE ADVANTAGE OF EVERY OPPORTUNITY TODAY BRINGS.***

Do have a blessed and productive day!

DAY 07

GOD IS ALWAYS WORKING

As you step out today, here's a reminder of God's word to you from John 5:17 [NIV].

"But Jesus answered them, "My Father has been working until now [He has never ceased working], and I too am working."

Today's Bible verse is to encourage and remind you as you go through different challenges and hard times that have tried to discourage you that God is still working. Jesus in this verse reminds us as believers that God has been working and goes on to tell us that He also is working on our behalf to make our lives a sign and wonder to others. We see this in the earlier verses of John 5 when Jesus healed the paralyzed man at the pool of Bethesda who had been there for 38 years without anyone to help him get to the pool to be healed.

Jesus broke the status quo by healing the man on a Sabbath day and this was considered a serious breach in traditions by the Jewish leaders. However, Jesus used the opportunity to remind us that God will never stop working because of man-made traditions. Jesus will not hesitate to break the norm or the status quo on your behalf because he needs to fulfil his purpose in your life. Therefore, be encouraged by God's word to you today that your Heavenly Father is at work always.

Because he delights in your peace, joy, and prosperity.

Therefore, as you go about your daily business and activities today, be encouraged by today's Bible verse and let it bring hope and peace to your heart as you go that challenging and difficult situation in your work, marriage, business, education, children relationship, career etc. You might be going through one difficulty to another and you are wondering why God seems silent, be still and be at peace because as today's bible verse says (He wants you to know this, so that you can have confidence and trust in him) God has been working until now and Jesus is also working too – that is what I call double blessings for your trouble, hallelujah!

So, even though you might not feel or see God working right now in your situation does not mean he is not. I encourage you to pause and you will see that He is working on other areas of your lives that are not immediately obvious to you. This is why the Holyspirit is reminding you today through this word not to give up hope or feel helpless because your Heavenly Father who watches over you does not sleep nor slumber Psalm 121:4. Instead, he is always at work because he is working all things for our good no matter how seemingly hopeless or near impossible the situation is or looks. Romans 8:28 (AMP) says ***"And we know [with great confidence] that God [who is deeply concerned about us] causes all things to work together [as a plan] for good for those who love God, to those who are called according to His plan and purpose."***

Here are few scriptures to remind you that God is still working on your behalf:

Psalm 68:19 **"Blessed be the Lord, who daily bears our burden, The God who is our salvation. Selah."**

Phillipians1:6 ***"For I am confident of this very thing, that He who began a good work in you will perfect it until the day of Christ Jesus."*** No matter how pressured your situation feels, Never, forget that God is always working and never stops working on your behalf.

Do have a blessed and productive day!

IS THERE ANYTHING TOO HARD FOR GOD?

As you step out today, here's a reminder of God's word to you from Jeremiah 32:27 [NIV].

> *"I am the LORD, the God of all the peoples of the world. Is anything too hard (difficult) for Me".*

The [MSG] Translation says,
> *"Stay alert! I am God, the God of everything living. Is there anything I can't do?"*

Is there anything to hard or difficult for God to do? This is a Rhetorical question that God posed to Jeremiah in today's key verse and this is the same question I believe God is asking us again today as we face circumstances that we have no control over, situations that has us against the wall and makes us feel everything is over. Without a shadow of doubt, we know that nothing can ever be Impossible for the God of all mankind but the truth is sometimes we face difficult challenges that deep in our thoughts we wonder if our situation is hard or difficult for God to change.

So today, I ask you is there a promise that the Lord has made to you? Or is there a promise from His word that you are holding on to, but sometimes doubt and unbelief kicks in and you begin to question what you believe and what God has said to you because the days, months and years seem to go without any sign of what God has promised?

Guess what! You are not the only one in that situation. Remember Sarah, Abraham's wife (see Genesis 18:10-15) who God referred to as the mother of nations, even when she was without any child. She was also included in the Bible 'Hall of fame' Hebrews 11 as a great example of saints of old who had faith and here's what Hebrews 11:11 says about her ***"It was by faith that even Sarah was able to have a child, though she was barren and was too old. She believed that God would keep his promise."***

But prior to her believing in God, the Bible tells us that she allowed doubt to creep into her heart regarding the promise of a child that God made to her (read Genesis 18:9-13) and in Genesis 18:14 God asked the same question just as in today's key verse ***"Is anything too hard for the LORD? I will return to you at the appointed time next year, and Sarah will have a son."*** Sarah initially doubted because she considered and looked at her current state, i.e., her age, which was past the childbearing age and she felt it was impossible for her to have a child! Logical and medically her reasons were genuine and valid but what she forgot to include in her thinking was that she was dealing with a God that specializes in making the Impossible Possible, the I'M POSSIBLE GOD, Hallelujah!

God, however, saw her doubt which made Him ask her in Genesis verse 14 *"is there anything too hard for the Lord."* But in spite of her initial doubt, God fulfilled His word to her because He is a Promise Keeper. Like Sarah, I too have allowed doubt to slip in, making me silently wonder if God can make a way in a situation that seem impossible to God but because God is a promise keeper and a respecter of his word.

Yes, what I ask him for may take months and in some instance years but again and again I have seen him honor his word in my life and truly reminded me that nothing is too hard or difficult for him to do. There are some things He has promised that I am still trusting him for, but I also choose to have faith like Sarah that He will bring to pass in due season.

So, today God is asking you too [insert your name] *"Is there anything too difficult for me to do?"* Concerning that business, career, marriage, job, child (ren), job, ministry, immigration issue etc. If God has promised you His blessings in any area of your life, just keep holding on, no matter how difficult and bleak the situation looks. Just like it was later said of Sarah in Hebrews 11 that she had faith and believed God. I want to believe that Sarah got to a place where she reflected on all God had done for them prior to that time that gave her the confidence assurance that a God truly was a promise keeper and as such Nothing was Impossible for him to do. I encourage you today to also intentionally choose to trust God and be dogged in your belief and faith in your Heavenly father to bring His promises to fulfilment in your life.

If God indeed promised you then know that He will bring it to pass in the due season. God speaking in Psalm 89:34 [KJV] also says **"My covenant will I not break, nor alter the thing that is gone out of my lips"**.

Therefore, as you go about your daily business and activities today, remind yourself and be assured in the truth of God's word that nothing is too big, difficult, complicated or impossible for your God to do. There is always a due season and an appointed time for God to fulfil His promise (s) to you. So, keep focused, keep your eyes fixed on the Lord and watch Him bring that promise to pass in your life in Jesus name. Again, don't forget, even if you can't see or don't feel God working, the truth is He is working. He never stops working because He neither slumbers nor sleeps (Psalm 121). And as such, He is working behind the scenes making sure His promises to you becomes a reality.

Remember, God always keeps to His words because He is not a man to lie! His promises are yes and Amen.

Do have a blessed and productive day!

DAY 09

LOADED WITH DAILY BENEFITS

As you step out today, here's a reminder of God's word to you from Psalm 68:19 [KJV].

"Blessed be the Lord, who daily loadeth us with benefits, even the God of our salvation. Selah."

The [AMPC] translation says,

"Blessed be the Lord, Who bears our burdens and carries us day by day, even the God Who is our salvation! Selah [pause, and calmly think of that]!"

Praise God! Today's key verse is such a beautiful reminder of God's unconditional love for us and how as a loving Father, He is always looking out for our best interests! It is a refreshing scripture because it reminds us as God's children that we are never alone because God is with us every step of the way even when we don't seem to sense His presence around us.

So, pause and calmly think of all the many burdens and situations God sees you through each day – too numerous to count!

Today's Bible verse also paints a picture in my mind of Santa, the gift sharing bearded man that has a gift for every child at Christmas time. For those who enjoy holiday movies, we get to see Santa and his elves in those movies working day and night tirelessly to meet children Christmas requests. They get busy selecting and wrapping the gifts so that they can get them delivered to the children who are excitedly and patiently waiting on Christmas day to unwrap the gift from Santa!

But glory be to God because the gifts (which signifies blessings) that God delivers to us is not limited to once a year but provided to us daily! Our God who neither sleeps nor slumbers (Psalm 121:4) works tirelessly all year round (24/7, 365days) wrapping up gifts specific to our needs (which includes provision, protection, mercies, miracles, answered prayers, healings, wisdom, favor to many to count) signed and sealed, delivered to us!

Our blessings are double dose because not only does God load us with many daily benefits (that money cannot buy) He also bears our burdens and carries us day by day through every situation we might be going through in our lives! Because sometimes when we go through challenges and difficulties, we start to wonder if God is indeed with us and often the devil takes advantage of those moments to sow seeds of doubt in our hearts.

Therefore, as you go about your daily business and activities today, walk consciously in your authority as a believer so that you can take advantage of the many benefits this day has for you. Make declarations and confessions regarding what you want to see today in your home, business, work, etc. because God's has so many benefits laid up for you 'today' in those areas of your life. God has worked so hard to prepare and release His blessings to you this day, so claim every one of them!

Remember, in between all you do today, pause for a few minutes and just utter *"Thank you, Heavenly Father, for your daily benefits poured out so lavishly unto me."*

Do have a blessed and productive day!

DAY 10

GOD'S FAVOR LASTS A LIFETIME

As you step out today, here's a reminder of God's word to you from Psalm 30:5 [NLT].

> *"For his anger lasts only a moment, but his favor lasts a lifetime! Weeping may last through the night, but joy comes with the morning."*

The MSG translation says,
> *"He gets angry once in a while, but across a lifetime there is only love. The nights of crying your eyes out give way to days of laughter."*

Today's key verse contains two important truth about God's love and faithfulness. The first part of this verse is a beautiful reminder of the characteristics of our Heavenly Father and I love how the scripture puts it that God's anger for us his children last just for a moment, i.e. just for a little while. I believe it's because God cannot permit Himself to be angry with us his children for more than a moment and this is because of his unlimited and unconditional love for us!

I also believe God's anger is really from a place of love as God cannot stand sin which is one thing that might make God to be upset with us. Habakkuk 1:13a says that God's eyes are too pure to look on evil and He cannot tolerate wrongdoing. God is Holy and wants us to be likewise as **1 Peter 1:15 says "But just** *as he who called you is holy, so be holy in all you do (you also be holy in all your conduct)."* God promises us through his word that he will not allow his anger towards us go for more than a moment and that is a reassurance to us that even when we fall short of his glory as Romans 3:23 says that *"For everyone has sinned; we all fall short of God's glorious standard."* God will forgive us when we ask for his forgiveness (1John 1:5).

We are confident that God's love for us is forever and supersedes his anger and this allows or affords us the privilege of coming boldly before his throne to receive mercy and find grace in time of need (Hebrews 4:16). This second part of today's verse points us to God's faithfulness and promise that joy is coming to every situation that has caused us to cry. God's promise of joy relates to every area of our lives that has brought us some form of pain or is causing us some sort of distress.

Therefore, as you go about your daily business and activities today, be confidence in this – that God's anger can only be for a moment towards you. And if you have been convicted by the Holyspirit of any wrongdoings or an area of sin, ask the Father for forgiveness, believe He has forgiven you and receive his love and favor that He extends to you for a lifetime. God is also saying to you through his word that no matter what you might be going through right now that has caused you to weep or causes you to shed tears through the night, Joy springs forth to you this morning in Jesus name! Hallelujah.

Remember, God's favor is for a lifetime!

You will testify to God's love, faithfulness, joy, and favor that will stand you out from others in Jesus name.

Do have a blessed and productive day!

DAY 11

GOD HAS A PLAN FOR YOU

As you step out today, here's a reminder of God's word to you from Jeremiah 29:11 [KJV].

"For I know the plans I have for you," declares the Lord, "plans to prosper you and not to harm you, plans to give you hope and a future."

The [NET Bible] translation says,

"I know what I have planned for you,' says the LORD. 'I have plans to prosper you, not to harm you. I have plans to give you a future filled with hope."

Today's key verse requires a little more time of your meditation because every word in this verse reveals the mind of God towards us His children. God loves us so much and His word reveals the extent of His love for us. God created us for a purpose. We are no accident or a thought after. God was intentional about bringing you to the scene and He reminds you through His word in case you have forgotten and have been so laden with life pressures and challenges that **HE HAS A PLAN FOR YOU!** God never speaks empty words, neither does He make a promise that He is unable to keep! Every word that God speaks is a done deal right from the moment He utters the word. Therefore, if God says He has plans to prosper you and me and to give us a future filled with hope. Then that is exactly what He is going to happen, no matter what we might have gone through or might be going through right now.

God is very intentional about His word because the bible says He exalts His word above His name (Psalm 138:2). When it comes to speaking about your purpose, God never jokes which means it is important that as a child of God you believe every word that God has spoken about you in His word and that is what Faith is all about, believing God's word. It is in believing God's word as the absolute truth that you truly enjoy the miracles and blessings that dwells in the word.

You might be going through very challenging and difficult situations right now, situations that threaten your peace and is in opposite direction of everything that God has promised you through His word. And you are beginning to doubt and almost believing the lie the devil is speaking to your mind that God does not have any good plans for you, neither does He have any plan for a future filled with hope and that there's really not any good plans that God has for you.

Let me remind you that this is a lie of the devil, a lie from the pit of hell itself. It is a lie because the devil is unable to speak the truth. In John 8:44 [NIV], the bible says concerning Satan, ***"He was a murderer from the beginning, not holding to the truth, for there is no truth in him. When he lies, he speaks his native language, for he is a liar and the father of lies."***

Know this – It is impossible for the devil to speak the truth because his DNA is lie in itself, which means all he's speaking to you and feeding you with are all lies. He speaks lies to us as believers and this leads to doubt and fear because He knows when we believe God's word we come into the fulfilment of

God's promises for our lives. So, it is time to shut him up with God's word to you today from Jeremiah 29:11. Hallelujah!

It's time to get radical with your confession and declaration and stop every voice of doubt and fear. We are grateful to God for his promise in today's key verse tucked beautifully in the Bible. A promise which when we wholeheartedly believe, has the power to ignite hope in us as believers especially in times when discouragement, uncertainty, fear, worry, insecurity, hopelessness, and doubt tries to eat deep at us.

Therefore, as you go about your daily business and activities today, take time to ponder and meditate on this scripture, confess and believe what God's word says to you. Keep pressing in on all that God has called you to do in every area of your life. Don't give up on all that God is leading you to do, no matter the obstacles and challenges you face. Keep going and keep being a blessing to people along the way and as you faithfully walk in obedience to God's word, you will see everything come together and the glorious future God has for you will unfold!

Remind the situation and circumstances that you might be going through today that against all odds you will choose to believe God's word because He never lies and its impossible for Him to lie. God's word never returns to Him void, NEVER! God's word never returns to Him empty; it accomplishes the purpose for which it was sent [Isaiah 55:11]. Know this -No matter how bleak, fuzzy or uncertain you feel about your future, God is reminding you through His word today that ***HE HAS A PLAN FOR YOU!***

Remember, God's plan for you is a future filled with hope and to give you an expected end, that is the ***ABSOLUTE TRUTH*** and you must choose to believe it. I pray you will see the fulfilment of God's purpose for your life in Jesus name, Hallelujah!

Do have a blessed and productive day!

DAY 12

A SONG OF GOD'S UNFAILING LOVE

As you step out today, here's a reminder of God's word to from Psalm 59:16-17 [NLT].

"But as for me, I will sing about your power. Each morning I will sing with joy about your unfailing love. For you have been my refuge, a place of safety when I am in distress. O my Strength, to you I sing praises, for you, O God, are my refuge, the God who shows me, unfailing love."

The [NLT] Translation says,
*"But I will sing of your strength, in the morning I will sing of your love; for you
are my fortress, my refuge in times of trouble. You are my strength;
I sing praise to you; you, God, are my fortress, my God on whom I can rely".*

The [AMP] Translation says,
*"But as for me, I will sing of Your mighty strength and power;
Yes, I will sing joyfully of Your loving kindness in the morning;
For You have been my stronghold*

And a refuge in the day of my distress.
To You, O [God] my strength, I will sing praises;
For God is my stronghold [my refuge, my protector, my high tower], the God who shows me [steadfast] lovingkindness."

Glory be to God! It's another beautiful day that the Lord has made. What a joy and a blessing to be alive and to be infused with the strength of the Lord to go about the daily activities that we need to accomplish today.

Reading through today's Bible verses, I am reminded of the beautiful lyrics of the song, '*I COULD SING OF YOUR LOVE FOREVER*', by the gospel singer Delirious

"Over the mountains and the sea,
Your river runs with love for me,
And I will open up my heart
And let the healer set me free.
I'm happy to be in the truth,
And I will daily lift my hands:
For I will always sing of when
Your love came down.

I could sing of your love forever,
I could sing of your love forever,
I could sing of your love forever,
I could sing of your love forever.
I could sing of your love forever.

Oh, I feel like dancing
It's foolishness I know;
But when the world has seen the light,
They will dance with joy"

Today's Bible verses reflect an attitude of complete trust in a God that can be trusted. A God that never fails. A mighty God who is in a class of his own, a class that cannot never be matched by anyone. An attitude of gratitude that leads to an outburst of praise, worship, and thanksgiving, hallelujah! As believers, we definitely have a lot to learn from King David when it comes to praising God even when the circumstances are far from perfect. This is because when David came up with this song, he was being pursued by King Saul's men to be killed. Yet, in all of this, King David maintained a heart of thanksgiving and saw around him many reasons to be grateful to God. So, just like King David, are there still many reasons for you to thank God despite your current challenges, the prayers that seemed not to be answered 'yet' or the many difficulties times you might have experienced recently?

Therefore, as you go about your daily business and activities today, take some moment to reflect on all of God's goodness, his unending love to you, His unfailing mercies to you and your loved ones throughout this year and year gone past. Yes, no doubt, it might have been a very rough couple of years for you or even this year might have dealt with you challenges you didn't expect or envisage. Regardless of all, you've been through, I encourage you today to give yourself permission to deliberately and intentionally sing of God's love, strength, mercies, peace, and his great faithfulness that are new every morning. Remind yourself in all you that He is your strength at all times, your dependable refuge, your fortress and a place of safety when in trouble.

Never forget that He is your ever reliable and dependable God, a very loving Father that can be trusted at all times and has never been known or heard to fail on any of His promises to His beloved children (i.e. you and me) Never! So, let praises burst out from your mouth in all that you do just like King a David and No matter what you might be going through, don't stop talking to the Lord about it because His ears are close to yours and He is excited to hear from His beloved, Hallelujah!

Do have a blessed and productive day!

DAY 13

NO RETREAT NO SURRENDER

As you step out today, here's a reminder of God's word to you from 2 Corinthians 4:16-18 [MSG].

> *16-18 "So we're not giving up. How could we! Even though on the outside it often looks like things are falling apart on us, on the inside, where God is making new life, not a day goes by without his unfolding grace. These hard times are small potatoes compared to the coming good times, the lavish celebration prepared for us. There's far more here than meets the eye. The things we see now are here today, gone tomorrow. But the things we can't see now will last forever."*

No retreat No surrender – this must be our stand position and watch word as believers at all times especially when the enemy of our soul, the devil tries to come into our territory.

Today's Bible verses are infused with hope geared at boosting our faith at the same time helping to keep our hearts stayed on the Lord even as we go through diverse challenges, difficult situations, life pressures, trials and troubles.

Ever watched one of those action packed movies especially the ones where you see an army preparing for war against an enemy or a football team going to take on a much stronger team? As you watch you get to that part of the scene that is likely to get you reflecting, or if you are like me you get to the part where you shed a tear and or get all pumped up with excitement as you listen to the coach/commander give a motivational speech to boost the confidence of the team for victory. An inspiring speech/message that not only gives the team of footballers or soldiers a sense of pride but also aimed at increasing their chance for success and victory. And this inspires in the people a 'can do' attitude and mind-set that influences everything they do as they face their giants.

Apostle Paul as a custodian of God's word who also like an army commander giving a motivational speech challenges the believers of his time and also challenges us still today that as God's enlisted soldier, we cannot afford to give up because of life troubles.

This is because Apostle Paul was not a man without his many shares of troubles, sorrows and sufferings as the Bible records, but he faithfully continued to passionately encourage the church and to also share the amazing love and grace of God to the unbelieving gentiles of his day.

So, for a man who understands pain and suffering in various dimensions, he is definitely not trying to trivialise our pain, suffering or troubles. Instead what he is doing is to redirect our focus & redefine our perspective so that we can see our trials just the same way our Heavenly Father sees them 'light and momentary' that are achieving for us an eternal glory that far outweighs all that we will ever go through, Hallelujah!

Apostle Paul is also challenging us through this scripture as believers called into a life of faith and trust in the Lord and as a people drafted into God's army that we cannot afford to give up or give in to our troubles, challenges and life pressures because we have victory in Christ Jesus.

He further reminds us that in midst of our challenges especially when it looks like things are crumbling and falling apart on us, on the inside, God is working in us strength of character and patience which is bringing about new life within us. And what joy to know that even in our trials not a day goes by without his unfolding grace revealed to us in everything we do.

Apostle Paul challenges us to look beyond the now and to set our eyes like flint on Jesus the author and finisher of our faith. To give our attention to the God of all hope, the one who gives us strength with his great power so that we don't give up when trouble comes.

I love how the Message translation puts it in verse 17, it says **"These hard times are small potatoes compared to the coming good time."** Don't you just want to shout Glory and do some Holy Ghost dance to let the devil know that you are more than a conqueror? hallelujah! I encourage you to pause and ponder on this scripture for few minutes because it offers the right perspective to view your situations reminding you that you are bigger than the situation regardless of how the devil tries to make you believe this is a gigantic problem.

David definitely demonstrated this overcomer's attitude when he saw Goliath like 'a small potato' and confronted him saying: *"Who is this uncircumcised Philistine that he should defy the armies of the living God?" (1*Samuel 17:26, you can read the whole account in the chapter).

Therefore, as you go about your daily business and activities today, be encouraged by the charge given by Apostle Paul to us all as believers to not give in or quit because we belong to a kingdom of dominion and we have been enlisted to an army that does not retreat or surrender. So in whatever challenging (or valley of the shadow of death) situation, you might be experiencing at the moment whether in your marriage, relationship, work, business, family, ministry, education, etc. which God knows and sees.

Remember, you are not alone because the Bible tells us God is with you every step of the way. He will not cause you to be disgraced or pit to shame, never! So yes even though on the outside it may often look like things are falling apart on you, never forget that on the inside, God is making a new life and perfecting you to make your sign, a wonder and blessing. And never forget that not a day goes by without his unfolding grace released towards you.

So, today say to yourself, "I am not giving up, I am not giving in. I am going to keep pressing in because there is NO RETREAT, NO SURRENDER because God has got me and I have total Victory in Christ Jesus, hallelujah!"

Do have a blessed and productive day!

DAY 14

GOD IS COMMITTED TO YOU

As you step out today, here's a reminder of God's word to you from Isaiah 30:21 [NLT] [NIV].

"Your own ears will hear him. Right behind you, a voice will say, "This is the way you should go," whether to the right or to the left."

"Whether you turn to the right or to the left, your ears will hear a voice behind you, saying, "This is the way; walk in it".

Today's Bible verse is in two parts. First, it reminds you and me as believers of the importance of hearing from God for ourselves.

Secondly, it gives us an assurance as believers that we are never alone because God promises through his word that whichever way we go He is always there with you and me. And this means that **GOD IS COMMITTED TO YOU!**

Hearing from God is very crucial and important as a believer because it helps you to be in God's will for your life at all times especially as it relates to you making decisions that impact your life, family, career, business, ministry, education etc. When you make hearing God a priority you can be sure that God will seek to always speak to you because He knows how much His word and hearing from Him means to you.

Today, you might have walked a path that has to lead you to regrettable places but God is reminding you that right where you are if you call out to him, He will speak to you and he will lead you along with new paths. God loves you unconditionally and He is always looking out for your welfare, yet God will never come in between your free will. God wants you to willingly put your trust in him and seek his wisdom and direction in all you do.

God doesn't want to be second place in your life, No, He doesn't and you know why? Because He is a jealous God. Yes God is jealous when it comes to us his children. The Bible puts it this way in Exodus 34:14 [NLT], it says ***"You must worship no other gods, for the LORD, whose very name is Jealous, is a God who is jealous about his relationship with you."*** In essence what God desires from us as his children is to place him first over everything in your life, to give him first place in our lives. He wants to take the center stage all the time.

Therefore, as you go about your daily business and activities, let your desire to hear God be your priority. A wise man preacher once said that "the truest thing you will hear about yourself say is what God has said to you" so make hearing from God one of your top priorities alongside knowing God more intimately.

You may wonder how do you hear from God or how do you recognise God's voice? Just as you recognise the voices of your loved ones because you have spent time with them. So, also will God's voice be recognizable in your spirit when you spend time in His word and in prayer (which is where you communicate with God and God communicate back to you).

My encouragement to you again is to be sensitive to the Holyspirit i.e. his leading and direction as you make decisions. Rely on His guidance and allow him to be your senior partner as He leads you in line with the Lord's will for your life in all that you do.

> *Remember, your ability to hear from God for yourself will always lead to blessing not just only for yourself but to many others too.*

Do have a blessed and productive day!

DAY 15

IN HIM WE LIVE, MOVE AND HAVE OUR BEING

As you step out today, here's a reminder of God's word to you from Acts 17:24-29 [Message] with emphasis on verse 28.

> *24-29 "The God who made the world and everything in it, this Master of sky and land, doesn't live in custom-made shrines or need the human race to run errands for him as if he couldn't take care of himself. He makes the creatures; the creatures don't make him.*
>
> *Starting from scratch, he made the entire human race and made the earth hospitable, with plenty of time and space for living so we could seek after God, and not just grope around in the dark but actually find him. He doesn't play hide-and-seek with us. He's not remote; he's near.*
>
> *We live and move in him, can't get away from him! One of your poets said it well: 'We're the God-created.' Well, if we are the God-created, it doesn't make a lot of sense to think we could hire a sculptor to chisel a god out of stone for us, does it?*

The English Standard Version translation of Verse 28 says *"**For In him we live and move and have our being**'; as even some of your own poets have said, "For we are indeed his offspring.'*

Today's Bible verses carefully explain the Sovereignty of God, the credentials of God and reminds us that as human beings our existence is solely dependent on him because ***IN HIM WE MOVE, LIVE AND HAVE OUR BEING!***

The central focus of this scripture reminds us that we don't exist just for ourselves but we are God-created for a purpose. And when we have that understanding we will choose to live life with more intentionality.

When you have the understanding that you don't exist just for yourself and that you can't get away from God, it will help you put your existence into perspective and make you set your priorities right every day.

Therefore, as you go about your daily business and activities today, let this scripture set you in motion to re-evaluate your priorities. Are your priorities set to honor God and to add value to the people around you and those you come in contact with daily?

Know this – you are God's creation and as a believer, redeemed and sanctified by the blood of Jesus Christ you are now His offspring and as such your life and everything you seek to do should always bring glory to God.

Remember, as a child of God you don't live for your own existence, you are God created and this means that your Identity now is in Christ.

God knows your every move and infact he knows the number of your days (Job 14:5) so let this verse echo within you always reminding you to make decisions and choices that reflects you as a light and salt to your sphere of influence.

Do have a blessed and productive day!

DAY 16

GOD'S WAYS ARE HIGHER

As you step out today, here's a reminder of God's word to you from Isaiah 55:9 [NLT].

"For just as the heavens are higher than the earth, so my ways are higher than your ways and my thoughts higher than your thoughts."

The [MSG] Translation says,

"I don't think the way you think. The way you work isn't the way I work." God's Decree."

Today's Bible verse, in a nutshell, indicates to us as believers God's *modus operandi* i.e. the way God works, His ways of doing things and the way He operates.

Ever wondered why God outlines His ways of operating to us? – I believe it's so that we can totally trust Him, have full confidence in Him and be at peace even as we go through hard and difficult times. Knowing that God has a great plan for us and will make sure that whatever we are going through works together for our good.

Our Heavenly Father is therefore, reminding us again today through this scripture that He is not a man and as such His dealings with us will never be based on human understanding.

As God's children, oftentimes go through some difficult challenges, situations and hard times, or we know believers that are going through difficult times that we struggle to understand why we or these believers have to go through this difficult situation/challenges/circumstances (Job is a man in the bible we can relate to in this situation).

It is important to remind ourselves as believers, that just as Jesus said in John 16:33 [AMP] *"I have told you these things, so that in Me you may have [perfect] peace. In the world, you have tribulation and distress and suffering, but be courageous [be confident, be undaunted, be filled with joy]; I have overcome the world." [My conquest is accomplished, My victory abiding.]"* We will go through challenging and faith shaking seasons.

But Christ through his word puts us at a better advantage over Satan (the enemy of our soul) because we know that we will go through different challenges in life but at the end of it we will come out victorious no matter how long it seems to take because our Lord Jesus has overcome the world, and that means everything is under his control. Hallelujah!

However, as believers, one thing we are often guilty of doing while we are going through this trials or tests is that there is a tendency for us to paint a picture in our mind or muse (i.e. consider thoughtfully) of how we want or feel God should come through for us (I guess our humanity kicks in sometimes, so let's no beat ourselves when we think like that). Or we try to suggest to God how to operate or best handle the situation, but the truth is God will never show up in the way we think He should.

Instead, He will show up in his own time, which is the right and perfect time and he would do it in such a way that only him will take the glory while it causes people to be in awe of His awesomeness, power, and might!

Therefore, as you go about your daily business and activities today, God wants you to know that because He has His own perfect ways, i.e. his modus operandi which is totally different from yours, He wants you to be at peace, not to worry, fret, be afraid or be anxious in that challenging situation you are going through or likely to go through because He is in charge. And when He is in charge, you can be sure that a Victory is ascertained!

Also, remember that there's a purpose in everything you have been through and are going through at the moment. God is very intentional with His dealings with you and me as his beloved children, and this explains why *His ways and thoughts are much higher than our ways and the way He thinks is so much different from the way we think*.

So, what God is doing in your life right now might not necessarily make sense to everybody around you, even to yourself but just know that there is a BEAUTIFUL STORY emerging from your life that will bless others and bring glory to God!

TODAY, CHOOSE TO TRUST TOTALLY IN GOD'S MODUS OPERANDI!

Do have a blessed and productive day!

DAY 17

DARE TO REMEMBER

As you step out today, here's a reminder of God's word to from Psalm 124:1-8 [AMP].

> *"If it had not been the Lord who was on our side,"*
> Let Israel now say,
> ² *"If it had not been the Lord who was on our side*
> *When men rose up against us,*
> ³ *Then they would have [quickly] swallowed us alive,*
> *When their wrath was kindled against us;*
> ⁴ *Then the waters would have engulfed us,*
> *The torrent would have swept over our soul;*
> ⁵ *Then the raging waters would have swept over our soul.*
> ⁶ *Blessed be the Lord,*
> *Who has not given us as prey to be torn by their teeth.*
> ⁷ *We have escaped like a bird from the snare of the*
> *fowlers; The trap is broken and we have escaped.*
> ⁸ *Our help is in the name of the Lord,*
> *Who made heaven and earth."*

"…I was 12 when I became an orphan… I buried my mama at 12 and in that moment, I felt lost, I felt my life was over as I no longer had anyone to run home to, no one to give me kisses, to celebrate my birthdays or watch me play games… I felt alone, abandoned and forsaken but in the midst of it all, I found God's love and I chose to trust him..."

As I listened to this young pastor share his testimony during church service, in that instance I was so overwhelmed with gratitude and I began to thank God for the privilege and huge opportunity He had given me and my husband to be alive to parent our children. In that moment I was deeply grateful for God's grace and mercies as I thought of my three amazing children and I just couldn't bring myself to think of their lives without us their parents.

Then in that moment, the Holyspirit casted my mind to years back when the enemy had tried to take me out prematurely. He attacked my mind by desperately trying to etch lies in my mind to believe I had an incurable disease (I still wonder how on Earth I even allowed that evil thought to gain grounds in my mind). That's why we must put 2 Corinthians 10:5 into action by ensuring that we cast down our every imagination, bringing into captivity every thought to the obedience of Christ.

The devil tried to torment me with the spirit of death such that I was always afraid to close my eyes to sleep. He also tried to plague me with a sickness that killed two friends that I knew but for El Elyon, I would have been taken out too by the devil. The one the Bible describes as the enemy that pursues our soul (Psalm 143:3) and whose full-time assignment and job description is to steal, kill and destroy (John 10:10).

I also remember when I had my firstborn in 2008 and a week later I was seated in my living room when I felt the urge to give out a deep cough and in the moment I did, in that very instance I felt my body expel out something from my lower part. I looked at it and it was lumps of blood clot.

Not sure what it was, I kept it to show my midwife on her visit to me and she was alarmed and sent me to emergency at the hospital because lo and behold they were remnants of the placenta inside of me. Later I was told by the midwife and also my mother who is also a midwife that the likely fatal consequences of what could have happened to me – Death … but for the Lord, He himself expelled this poison from within me.

And He did the same again in 2015 when after 12weeks I had a miscarriage, only to be told by the Doctor it was a missed miscarriage (this is when the foetus in the womb dies at about 6 weeks) again the Lord performed his surgery on me and made me expel this poison from within me at 12weeks. Oh! Had it not been the Lord, I would have been long gone – thank you Lord!

Today's Bible passage in a nutshell captures the goodness of the Lord in the lives of each and every one of us as his children. Each verse echoes our own testimony of God's goodness, mercies and faithfulness and without God's mighty hand upon our lives, our story would have been different!

Today's Bible verse is a challenge of gratitude for the Lord's goodness in our lives. A challenge to get us to dare to remember the victories the Lord has dealt so wondrously in our lives.

> So, yes ***"If it had not been the Lord who was on our side, If God hadn't been for us when everyone and everything went against us. We would have been swallowed alive, swallowed alive by the enemy's violent anger, swept away by the flood of rage, drowned in the torrent; we would have lost our lives in the wild, raging water....***

But hallelujah! ***Oh, blessed be God! He didn't go off and leave us. He didn't abandon us defenceless or leave us helpless as a rabbit in a pack of snarling dogs. We've flown free from their fangs, free of their traps, free as a bird. Their grip is broken; we're free as a bird in flight. God's strong name is our help, the same God who made heaven and earth.***" (MSG)

Therefore, as you go about your daily business and activities today, I encourage you to intentionally take out time and allow the Holyspirit to cast your mind back to moment(s) in the years past that the Lord wrought his miracle in your life.

Moments where you knew that if God had not showed up, your story would have been different today. It's time to dare to remember because had it not been the Lord on your side," the enemy would have made a feast of you! (Paraphrased).

Do have a blessed and productive day!

DAY 18

THE KINGDOM RELATIONSHIP CYCLE

As you step out today, here's a reminder of God's word to you from Isaiah 60:1-2 [NIV].

"Arise, shine, for your light has come, and the glory of the LORD rises upon you.

²See, darkness covers the earth, and thick darkness is over the peoples, but the LORD rises upon you, and his glory appears over you."

This is God's clarion call and mandate to us as His children to **ARISE** and to **SHINE** so that we can declare His glory in the nations of the earth!

Being a Light means that you have been empowered by God to bring hope, joy, love, good tidings, deliverance, solutions, etc. to those around you. When we walk in love, or we demonstrate the fruits of the Holyspirit to those around us, this means we are Shinning the light of Christ in us!

One of our core assignments as a child of God is to be a LIGHT and what light does is to bring illumination to areas of darkness. The world we live in today is characterised by so much darkness and evil and like never before the light of

Christ which we carry as God's children are required.

The Bible says in verse two that darkness, i.e., gross darkness covers the earth and we can testify to that gross darkness with all that is happening in our world today. But because God has called us to be light bearers we are empowered and commissioned by Him to dispel the darkness around us. God has called and has placed a mandate on us His children to Arise in every sphere of influence He has placed us in to shine the light of His Kingdom.

Ephesians 2:10 tells us that as God's handiwork we are created in Christ for good works. And our good works represents Light and Hope that we bring to people, communities, and nations. Therefore, because you are a child of God, you are light just as Christ is LIGHT (John 8:12).

As you go about your daily business and activities today, remember that Christ depends on you and me to Arise and Shine our lights to the darkness (which can come in the form of people's ignorance, unkindness, selfishness, unbelief in Christ, wickedness and all sorts of evil) around us. And by doing this the glory of our Lord Jesus is risen and seen in the life of people. Halleluyah!

Remember, light, no matter how little it shines, it has the capacity has to dispel darkness so, ARISE and SHINE.

Do have a blessed and productive day!

DAY 09

ENTER THE PASSWORD — THANK YOU

As you step out today, here's a reminder from God's word to you from – Psalm 100:1-5 [MSG].

> *¹⁻² "On your feet now—applaud God!*
> *Bring a gift of laughter,*
> *sing yourselves into his presence.*
> *³ Know this: God is God, and God, God.*
> *He made us; we didn't make him.*
> *We're his people, his well-tended sheep.*
> *⁴ Enter with the password: "Thank you!"*
> *Make yourselves at home, talking praise.*
> *Thank him. Worship him.*
> *⁵ For God is sheer beauty,*
> *all-generous in love,*
> *loyal always and ever."*

The NLT translation says,

> *"^{1.}Shout with joy to the LORD, all the earth! ^{2.}Worship the LORD with gladness. Come before him, singing with joy. ^{3.}Acknowledge that the LORD is God! He made us, and we are his. We are his people, the sheep of his pasture. ^{4.}Enter his gates with thanksgiving; go into his courts with praise. Give thanks to him and praise his name.*

⁵"For the LORD is good. His unfailing love continues forever, and his faithfulness continues to each generation."

'ENTER WITH THE PASSWORD – THANK YOU'

Wow! Isn't it awesome to know that this is all that is required for you and me as a child of God to gain access into the very presence of our loving, Heavenly Father and to gain an audience with him! Today's key verses admonish us to come into God's presence to give thanks, to bring a gift of laughter, to shout with joy to the lord, to give praises to our Heavenly Father because he made us, and we are his and to sing ourselves into his presence. Today's Bible verses also remind us that God's unfailing love and faithfulness continues from one generation to another.

Therefore, as you go about your daily business and activities today, let gratitude and thankfulness flow from your heart to the Lord because He is a good and loving Father who cares for you and whose love for you is everlasting. Don't let your current challenges hinder you from worshipping the Lord with gladness in your heart. Yes, you might say to yourself "it's really so difficult to thank God right now because my situation remains unchanged"

But here's what you should reflect on – Christ did not say you would not go through trials, troubles, and tribulations – yes you and me will go through so many while we are here on earth but He did assure you to be of good cheer because He has OVERCOME the world (John 16:33). There's breath in you today, then that's a good place to start with, in praising God. So, today acknowledge God's faithfulness, goodness, kindness, mercies, protection of you and your loved ones.

Remember God's grace and mercies have kept you through the years and through every season of life and for that you want to shout with joy in praise and thanksgiving to his holy name! So, today, intentionally set your mind to focus on that aspect of your life that is worth praising God for and take your time to count your blessings – and don't forget the password to his presence is THANK YOU.

Do have a blessed and productive day!

DAY 20

COME BODLY TO THE THRONE OF GRACE

As you step out today, here's a reminder of God's word to you from Hebrews 4:16 [NLT].

> *"So let us come boldly (with confidence) to the throne of our gracious God. There we will receive his mercy, and we will find grace to help us when we need it most."*

The NIV translation says,

> *"Let us then approach God's throne of grace with confidence, so that we may receive mercy and find grace to help us in our time of need."*

Today's key verses is a special invitation, infact more like a love letter from God directed to us His children letting us know that we are always welcome to come before His throne of Grace.

Think for a moment, why is this throne called the **THRONE OF GRACE?** From my study of the scriptures over the years, I know it is called the throne of grace because there's no accusation, no shaming, and no condemnation. I also believe it's called the throne of Grace because of the price our savior Jesus Christ paid for us on the cross of Calvary. Christ death on the cross not only gave us victory over sin.

It also gave us direct access to God's throne, and His death released God's grace (a free, undeserved, generous and spontaneous gift from God made possible by Christ death and resurrection) to us which we now have access to enjoy freely.

As Ephesians 2:8 explains that it is by grace we have been saved because it's a free gift of God, which means you and me cannot boast or take credit for it.

Therefore, as you go about your daily business and activities, God is personally inviting you this morning and every day to come unashamedly to his throne of Grace with confidence so that you can fellowship with him and while you are doing that, you are overwhelmed with His love, grace, favour, and mercy.

It is refreshing to know that God's word is an assurance to us that He cares for us and that He has our best interest at heart. God's word indeed brings joy to our soul and also makes provision for every area of our lives.

Remember that no matter the situation or challenges you are going through today, you don't have to go through it alone. God is waiting for you to come with boldness and confidence before His throne so He can listen to you and empower you with all that you need to overcome that situation!

Believe and meditate on God's word and let it be the anchor for your soul! Remember God is bound by His word Isaiah 55:10-11 and He is too full of integrity to break any of it.

Do have a blessed and productive day!

DAY 21

INTENTIONAL FRIENDSHIP

As you step out today, here's a reminder of God's word to you from Proverbs 18:24 [MSG].

> *"Friends come and friends go, but a true friend sticks by you like family."*

The NLT Translation says,
> *"There are "friends" who destroy each other, but a real friend sticks closer than a brother."*

The [GWT] translation says,
> *"Friends can destroy one another, but a loving friend can stick closer than family."*

The [AMP] Translation says,
> *"The man of too many friends [chosen indiscriminately] will be broken in pieces and come to ruin, but there is a [true, loving] friend who [is reliable and] sticks closer than a brother."*

Today's Bible verse expresses the importance of friendship and the blessing that lies in true friendship i.e. a friendship void of every hidden motive. Today's Bible verse also emphasizes the need for us as believers to intentionally seek opportunities to cultivate a friendship that focuses on adding value to others.

A friendship relationship that is not aimed at destroying or pulling others down but a friendship relationship that is like family (a united one) that endeavours to cover the shame of others. A friendship relationship that is not based on unrealistic expectations but on agape love, mutual trust, understanding, sacrifices, genuine care and willing to go the extra mile even when not convenient. A friendship relationship that is not based on the desires of the flesh such as jealousy, greed, but a one that seeks to bring out the best in the other and seeks to speak the truth even when it hurts.

No doubt, true and loving friendship is a dire need in our 'broken' society of today as there are one to many relationships that exist for selfish interest (just about the benefits they can get out of the relationship) and to feed their ego. The news and social media's are daily filled with so many disturbing, heart-breaking, soul-wrenching, unbelievable news of what people do and unfortunately some of these involves relationship between family members.

This is why today's Bible verse is so apt as it clearly reveals the state of relationships in our world today. We live in times now that it is increasingly difficult to find authentic relationships where a friend sticks closer than a brother/sister or family. Infact, it is so sad to even see families destroy each other for (economic and selfish) reasons though this is not a surprise as the Bible state in 2Timothy3:2 that *"people will be lovers of self [narcissistic, self-focused], lovers of money [impelled by greed], boastful, arrogant, revilers, disobedient to parents, ungrateful, unholy and profane."*

This is why as believers; we have been given the mandate by God to be **salt and light.** Jesus said in Matthew 5:13-16

¹³. "You are the salt of the earth. But if the salt loses its saltiness, how can it be made salty again? It is no longer good for anything, except to be thrown out and trampled underfoot.

¹⁴. "You are the light of the world … ¹⁶. In the same way, let your light shine before others, that they may see your good deeds and glorify your Father in heaven."

This means that as believers we are committed to living a life of doing good and making sure that the relationships, we build adds value and brings out the best in them. There is no true and real covenant friendship without sacrifices, and we see that in the life of David and Jonathan who were covenant friends (1Samuel chapters 18-20), a relationship that clearly exemplifies today's Bible verse.

I remember in my teens, I had so many friends because I found it quite easy to make friends and to start a conversation with even strangers. I realized growing up that being friendly and engaging quickly with acquaintances was one of my key strengths. However, now as an adult, a believer and a student of God's word, I understand that friendship needs to be intentional and deliberate for it to be meaningful. So, I am more **conscious, deliberate, and intentional** of my role now in every relationship I find myself that spans beyond being an acquaintance. I understand that I have to be committed to adding value to that relationship and knowing that it will require many sacrifices too.

Lest not forget that every good and healthy relationship is dyadic i.e. a two-way relationship, so it is good to take a review of your relationships today especially as we come to the end of 2017. If it is a one-sided relationship and one that constantly or continually drains you, I think it is about time you let go of that relationship and prayerfully trust God for a covenant relationship that would add value to you!

Therefore, as you go about your daily business and activities today, make up your mind to be the friend that Proverbs 18:24 talks about and to also prayerfully seek out (covenant) friends that can also be the Proverb 18:24 friend to you. The world desperately needs such type of covenant friendship. Also, take time to read about the amazing covenant relationship between David and Jonathan (1Samuel 18) so that you have a model of what real covenant friendship looks like so this can be your template of what your relationships will be built upon for it to be healthy!

To be a friend that sticks closer than a brother/sister/family requires your time, commitment and sacrifice. You don't have to do it in your own strength or power, but you can ask the Holyspirit to strengthen and give you grace to be such blessed friend.

Do have a blessed and productive day!

DAY 22

GOD'S MODUS OPERANDI

As you step out today, here's a reminder of God's word to you from Isaiah 55:9 [NLT].

> *"For just as the heavens are higher than the earth, so my ways are higher than your ways and my thoughts higher than your thoughts."*

The [MSG] Translation says,
> *"I don't think the way you think. The way you work isn't the way I work." God's Decree."*

Today's Bible verse, in a nutshell, indicates to us as believers God's *modus operandi* i.e. the way God works, His ways of doing things and the way He operates.

Ever wondered why God outlines His ways of operating to us? – I believe it's so that we can totally trust Him and be at peace even as we go through hard and difficult times. Our Heavenly Father is therefore, reminding us again today through this scripture that He is not a man and as such His dealings with us will never be based on human understanding. As God's children, oftentimes go through some difficult challenges, situations and hard times, or we know believers that are going through difficult times that we struggle to understand why we or these believers have to go through this difficult situation/challenges/circumstances (Job is a man in the bible we can relate to in this situation).

It is important to remind ourselves as believers, that just as Jesus said in John 16:33 [AMP] ***"I have told you these things, so that in Me you may have [perfect] peace. In the world, you have tribulation and distress and suffering, but be courageous [be confident, be undaunted, be filled with joy]; I have overcome the world." [My conquest is accomplished, my victory abiding.]"*** We will go through challenging and faith shaking seasons.

But Christ through his word puts us at a better advantage over Satan (the enemy of our soul) because we know that we will go through different challenges in life but at the end of it we will come out victorious no matter how long it seems to take because our Lord Jesus has overcome the world, and that means everything is under his control. Hallelujah!

However, as believers, one thing we are often guilty of doing while we are going through this trials or tests is that there is a tendency for us to paint a picture in our mind or muse (i.e. consider thoughtfully) of how we want or feel God should come through for us. Or we try to suggest to God how to operate or best handle the situation, but the truth is God will never show up in the way we think He should. Instead, He will show up in his own time, which is the right and perfect time and he would do it in such a way that only him will take the glory while it causes people to be in awe of His awesomeness, power, and might!

Therefore, as you go about your daily business and activities today, God wants you to know that because He has His own modus operandi which is totally different from yours, He wants you to be at peace, not to worry, fret, be afraid or be anxious in that challenging situation you are going through or likely to go through because He is in charge. And when He is in charge, you can be sure that a Victory is ascertained!

Also, remember that there's a purpose in everything you have been through and are going through at the moment. God is very intentional with His dealings with you and me as his beloved children, and this explains why *His ways and thoughts are much higher than our ways and the way He thinks is so much different from the way we think.*

So, what God is doing in your life right now might not necessarily make sense to everybody around you, even to yourself but just know that there is a BEAUTIFUL STORY emerging from your life that will bless others and bring glory to God!

TODAY, CHOOSE TO TRUST TOTALLY IN GOD'S MODUS OPERANDI!

Do have a blessed and productive day!

DAY 23

GOD HUMBLES THE PROUD AND THE HUMBLE HE HONORS

As you step out today, here's a reminder from God's word to you from Luke 18:10-14 [TLB].

"Then he told this story to some who boasted of their virtue and scorned everyone else:

[10] "Two men went to the Temple to pray. One was a proud, self-righteous Pharisee, and the other a cheating tax collector. 11 The proud Pharisee 'prayed' this prayer: 'Thank God, I am not a sinner like everyone else, especially like that tax collector over there! For I never cheat, I don't commit adultery, 12 I go without food twice a week, and I give to God a tenth of everything I earn.'

[13] "But the corrupt tax collector stood at a distance and dared not even lift his eyes to heaven as he prayed, but beat upon his chest in sorrow, exclaiming, 'God, be merciful to me, a sinner.' 14 I tell you, this sinner, not the Pharisee, returned home forgiven! For the proud shall be humbled, but the humble shall be honored."

Today's Bible reading is another parable told by Jesus to illustrate the need for us to be humble, not to judge others and definitely not to be so conceited that we place ourselves better than others.

James 4:6 also reiterate this statement by Jesus when it says

> *"...That is why Scripture says: "God opposes the proud but shows favor to the humble."*

Today's scriptural verses are very clear about God's view of pride, especially When it relates to us His children. God does not want us to be caught up in Pride. Jesus without mincing words in this parable firmly says, **"For the proud shall be humbled, but the humble shall be honored."**

We can't say we are Christ ambassadors, yet be so prideful and vain that people begin to question our character and if we are really what we say we are – Christians.

There are many verses in the Bible that address the issue of pride and its repercussions. Here are some few bible verses.

> *Romans 12:16 "Live in harmony with one another. Do not be proud but be willing to associate with people of low position. Do not be conceited" i.e. (Don't be too proud to enjoy the company of ordinary people. And don't think you know it all!*

> *"Philippians 2:3 "Do nothing from selfishness or empty conceit, but with humility of mind regard one another as more important than yourselves;"*

> *1Samuel 2:3 "Do not keep talking so proudly or let your mouth speak such arrogance, for the LORD is a God who knows, and by him, deeds are weighed."*

Psalm 75:5 "Do not lift up your horn on high, do not speak with insolent pride."

Proverbs 16:18 "Pride goes before destruction, and haughtiness before a fall."

1Peter 5:5 "All of you, clothe yourselves with humility toward one another, because, "God opposes the proud but shows favor to the humble."

Therefore, as you go about your daily business and activities today, let the words of Christ in this parable resonate within you, making you make up your mind daily to intentionally stay humble no matter the level of your success in life. Be conscious not to walk in Pride or think yourself more highly than others because pride is of the flesh and if not stopped, can lead to other forms of sin.

Note this – **Pride will draw and repel people away from you, leading to closed doors but humility will open the hearts of people towards you and keep the doors of opportunities opened constantly to you!**

Remember you are a Christ-Representer, so make sure your words match your actions. Be a man and woman of godly character wherever you go. So that even when people want to talk evil about you, it will be hard for them to pin pride and arrogance on you.

As Proverbs says Pride goes/comes before a fall, so stay humble always and remember God promises to show honor and favor to those that are humbled!

Do have a blessed and productive day!

DAY 24

LOVED WITH AN EVERLASTING LOVE, LOVED BY AN EVERLASTING FATHER

As you step out today, here's a reminder of God's word to you from Jeremiah 31:3 [MSG].

> *"God told them, "I've never quit loving you and never will. Expect love, love, and more love!"*

The World English Bible translation says,
> *"Yahweh ... [saying], Yes, I have loved you with an everlasting love: therefore, with lovingkindness have I drawn you."*

If you have ever been in doubt of God's love for you because you sometimes feel that you fall short of doing what God wants you to do, today's key verse is such a beautiful and amazing reminder of the unconditional love that God has for you and me.

God reminds us through this scripture that no matter the weaknesses in our lives that seem to make us feel unworthy of receiving God's love and grace, He as our loving Father has never and will never quit loving us rather what we can expect from is ***LOVE, LOVE, AND MORE LOVE. Hallelujah!!!***

Today's key verse is God's personal love letter to you, and He is reminding you this morning through his word that you are

LOVED WITH AN EVERLASTING LOVE i.e. a love that is pure, guilt-free, eternal and unchanging. Therefore do not let guilt, condemnation, the feeling of not being good enough, or the lies of the devil that no matter how much you try, you will never get it right or be good enough for God rob you of the truth that God loves you unconditionally.

The bible states in Romans 5:8 that *"God demonstrates and proves his own love for us in this: While we were still sinners, Christ died for us."*

God's love pursues us just like a groom pursues his bride. God longs to love us endlessly not only when we get it right but also when we fall short and don't get it right. God loves you and I 'recklessly' and He will do everything it takes to win us back to Him again and again. We see this love demonstrated in the parable of the prodigal son in Luke 15:11-32.

God's love for us is immeasurable, it is not conditioned only to a date, like February 14th (a day set aside to show love in a special way which sometimes is motivated by selfish reasons). God's love is pure, true and beautiful!

God's love for us can never fail, it can never run dry and it will never run out on us simply because God is committed to loving and not quitting loving us!

Therefore, as you go about your daily business and activities today, I would encourage you to take a moment to meditate and soak in this beautiful love lines that God is speaking to you through today's key verse. If you ever feel short of God's love (which is a lie the devil tries to sell to us as believers) just run to the Father's Mercy Seat.

Come boldly before your heavenly Father's throne of grace (Hebrews 4:16) where you can be assured that a Beautiful Exchange will take place where every feeling of inadequacy, condemnation, guilt, and weakness exists. Love up on your Father today, thank Him for His everlasting and unconditional love towards you and ask Him for renewed strength and grace to keep pursuing Him every day!

> ***Remember, you're Loved with an everlasting Love, loved by an everlasting God, so Expect love, love and More Love!***

Do have a blessed and productive day!

DAY 25

THERE IS A DUE SEASON – DON'T BE IMPATIENT

As you step out today, here's a reminder from God's word to you from Psalm 37:34 [TLB].

"Don't be impatient for the Lord to act! Keep traveling steadily along his pathway and in due season he will honor you with every blessing, and you will see the wicked destroyed."

… *"Don't be impatient"* This is a line that many times I find myself telling my children when they go on and on for me to get them something they desperately want. They want it in their own time but as a parent, I know there are many factors to consider, which will prolong the time, but they will eventually get it at the right time. I know many parents and guardians can sure relate to this :).

Don't we as believers do this too to our Heavenly Father when we come with our request (s), and just like our children we cry out, "we want it Now"! Today's key verse is a reminder to you and me as God's children on the importance of trusting God, patiently waiting on him and keeping our hearts stayed on Him even as we trust him for various needs in our lives. This is one scripture that has been a tremendous blessing to me in seasons where I find myself discouraged or anxious for God to step into a situation.

The Bible tells us that there are blessings stored up and reserved for us in Christ Jesus, however, patience is a key factor that we must be willing to exercise to lay hold of every blessing that God has for us in our family, relationship, marriage, career, ministry etc. Hebrews 10:36 says " ***Patient endurance is what you need now, so that you will continue to do God's will. Then you will receive all that he has promised.***"

The writer of today's verse encourages us as believers not to be impatient for the Lord to act on our behalf because he's truth is our Heavenly Father is working tirelessly to make all things work together for our good. This scripture also encourages us not give up in our service to the Lord because there is a **DUE SEASON** set out by the Lord to bless us if we don't give up. While we are waiting, God is working out things for our good and putting things in place for us, which is why we must trust him. God tells us in his word (Jeremiah 29:11) that he has great plans for us which he will bring to pass just at the right time!

God wants us to trust him and to keep trusting him in and out of season. And being patient is how we show God that we have firm confidence and believe in his sovereignty. As believers trust is crucial to receiving every promise God makes to us.

Therefore, as you go about your daily business and activities today, let this scripture reignite your commitment to trust God no matter what you go through. You have to be intentional about telling yourself that God loves and cares for you and loves you too recklessly to abandon or forsake you. This is a truth you must believe and own. Also, remind yourself that there is a **DUE SEASON** that God has set out to bless and honor you in regard to everything you are trusting him to do in your life and in the life of your loved ones.

But the admonition to you is not to be impatient. God is a rewarder of those that diligently seek him (Hebrews 11:6). Hebrews 10:23 also encourages us by saying *"Let us hold tightly without wavering, (unswervingly) to the hope we affirm, for God can be trusted to keep his promise."*

While you are patiently waiting for the Lord to act in that 'desperate and challenging situation' remember to still, thank him, worship him, keep loving him, keep loving people, keep serving and keep praising him!

And I encourage you to make this declaration below:

> *I won't be impatient for the Lord to act. I will keep travelling steadily along his pathway and in due season. He will honor with every blessing.*

Remember, God is faithful to his word, hallelujah.

Do have a blessed and productive day!

DAY 26

IT'S TIME TO QUIT WORRYING

As you step out today, here's a reminder of God's word to you from Matthew 5:25 -31 [TLB].

> ^{25} "So my counsel is: Don't worry about things—food, drink, and clothes. For you already have life and a body—and they are far more important than what to eat and wear. ^{26}Look at the birds! They don't worry about what to eat—they don't need to sow or reap or store up food—for your heavenly Father feeds them. And you are far more valuable to him than they are. ^{27}Will all your worries add a single moment to your life?

> ^{28}And why worry about your clothes? Look at the field lilies! They don't worry about theirs. ^{29}Yet King Solomon in all his glory was not clothed as beautifully as they. ^{30}And if God cares so wonderfully for flowers that are here today and gone tomorrow, won't he more surely care for you, O men of little faith?

> "$^{31\text{-}32}$"So don't worry at all about having enough food and clothing. Why be like the heathen? For they take pride in all these things and are deeply concerned about them. But your heavenly Father already knows perfectly well that you need them, ^{33}and he will give them to you if you give him first place in your life and live as he wants you to.

> **³⁴"So don't be anxious about tomorrow. God will take care of your tomorrow too. Live one day at a time."**

While on a trip abroad, I got talking to a young lady and whilst we engaged in an interesting conversation. She shared with me how she tends to worry a lot and then stated that she had definitely inherited worry from her mother who worried about every little thing. I could only imagine her mental well-being as worry impacts greatly on our mental state of mind.

Well, her statement got me thinking of how as believers (including myself) we often find ourselves worrying about so many things which may include but not limited to finances, marriage, bills, work, rent, life partners, mortgage, school fees, relationships, not failing, getting a job, education, children, spouses, ministry etc.

Not because we are not aware of what the scripture says about worry but because we often let down our guards by taking our focus away from Jehovah Jireh and focusing them on our circumstances and challenges.

So, a reality check right there for us. It's time to quit worrying! Do we worry so much that we have unconsciously passed or are passing on worry to our children & those that look up to us? It's time to quit worrying.

In today's key Bible verses, Jesus knowing how prone we are as human beings to worry about everything especially what to eat, drink and wear. Such that we forget the most important things – i.e. life and a body of which if we didn't have, worrying about what to eat and drink will then be totally irrelevant.

As Jesus began his public ministry, teaching and sharing the gospel to the multitudes that gathered around him. I find it interesting that with all the powerful teaching on various kingdom issues that Jesus shared to the crowd, He dedicated an ample time (about ten verses) to addressing the issue of worry and focusing our attention on the things that are important. Because Jesus knows that worry is a faith killer and a breeding ground for hopelessness, anxiety, unbelief, doubt which can then lead to lack of faith and total trust in God.

Jesus full of love for us as his children, want us to be free from worry and anxiety knowing that they steal our peace, joy and quality time with our Heavenly Father. Jesus therefore, lovingly tells us that God our Heavenly Father perfectly knows all that we need but we must first seek him, give his the first place in our lives, live as he wants us too, acknowledge him in all our ways and seek to do all that He desires of us.

Apostle Paul further reiterates this truth in Philippians 4:6 when he admonishes believers not to worry and instead provided a step by step action to take to counter worry and anxiety.

> *"Do not be anxious or worried about anything, but in everything [every circumstance and situation] by prayer and petition with thanksgiving, continue to make your [specific] requests known to God. 7 And the peace of God [that peace which reassures the heart, that peace] which transcends all understanding, [that peace which] stands guard over your hearts and your minds in Christ Jesus [is yours]."*

Therefore, as you go about your daily business and activities today, bear this truth from verse 34 in mind *"So don't be anxious about tomorrow. God will take care of your tomorrow too. Live one day at a time."*

Yes, even after reading this devotional, you might find yourself swamped up with potential 'worry' situations but I encourage you to etch God's word in your heart and mind and intentionally choose to put into practice what it says – Seek his kingdom first, by prayer and thanksgiving continue to make your specific requests to God.

Remember, God promises that He will give you all that you need only if you give him first place in your life and live as he wants you to. Don't get so 'deeply concerned 'about your needs that you relegate God to the side or take him out of the equation and lose faith in him. It's time to quit every form of worry in your life and family, speak to your soul today and say "I quit worrying and I choose to trust my heavenly father, who is the Sovereign God."

My Prayer for you
I pray that the Holyspirit will help us to continually put our trust in the Lord and in any area of our lives where there is worry, his peace, hope and joy will overtake in Jesus name.

Do have a blessed and productive day!

DAY 27

A PROMISE AND AN ASSURANCE

As you step out today, here's a reminder of God's word to you from Isaiah 41:10 [NLT].

> *"Don't be afraid, for I am with you. Don't be discouraged, for I am your God. I will strengthen you and help you. I will hold you up with my victorious right hand."*

Good News Translation;

> *"Do not be afraid–I am with you! I am your God–let nothing terrify you! I will make you strong and help you; I will protect you and save you."*

The NIV Translation says;

> *"So do not fear, for I am with you; do not be dismayed, for I am your God. I will strengthen you and help you; I will uphold you with my righteous right hand."*

Today's Bible verse is an assurance and a promise from God to you. God is reminding you of his word this morning as you go about your daily business and activities, for you:

NOT TO BE AFRAID

NOT TO TREMBLE IN FEAR

NOT TO BE DISMAYED

NOT TO GIVE UP HOPE

NOT TO FEEL WORTHLESS

NOT TO BE DISCOURAGED

God is aware of all that you are going through because He is the All-Knowing and the All-Seeing God. Nothing is hidden before Him.

God sees your many nights of crying, asking him to step into that challenging situation that is draining out your faith.

God knows your struggles. He is not oblivious to your pain, worry, and anxiety.

He knows how helpless you feel about not able to change your challenging situation.

Which is why God is saying to you this morning that:

HE WILL STRENGTHEN YOU

HE WILL HELP YOU

HE WILL PROTECT YOU

HE WILL SAVE YOU

HE WILL MAKE YOU STRONG

HE WILL GIVE YOU HOPE

HE WILL TURNAROUND YOUR CHALLENGING SITUATION AROUND FOR GOOD

AND HE WILL UPHOLD YOU WITH HIS RIGHTEOUS HAND

This is God's promise and assurance to you this morning. Believe it and thank Him for his promise to you. God is a promise keeper. Once He speaks, He fulfills his word.

So, put God's word from Today's Bible verse side by side to every challenging situation and declare the Victory that is yours in Jesus name!

Do have a blessed and productive day!

DAY 28

GOD'S WORD IS TRUTH AND LIFE

As you step out today, here's a reminder of God's word to you from Proverbs 3:5-8 [MSG].

> *"Trust God from the bottom of your heart;*
> *don't try to figure out everything on your own.*
> *Listen for God's voice in everything you do, everywhere you go;*
> *he's the one who will keep you on track.*
> *Don't assume that you know it all.*
> *Run to God! Run from evil!*
> *Your body will glow with health,*
> *your very bones will vibrate with life!"*

God's word is loaded with so much truth and wisdom that helps us to navigate each day's problem. God's word brings life and light into every area of darkness and if we heed His word, we can be certain of victory in every area of our lives! The truth is, obedience to God's word and laws is really for our own benefit and we will be doing ourselves as believers a lot of good when we adhere to his instructions.

Today's key verses are filled with life-giving instructions that will do us a lot of good only when we commit to doing what it instructs us to do.

Therefore, as you go about your daily business and activities, here is what the Holyspirit is saying to you to consider to do today and every day. That you should trust God from the bottom of your heart and totally trust him to handle the affairs of your life, family, children, marriage, business, career, ministry etc.

That you should not try to figure out everything on your own but allow Jesus to take the worry off you and cast your cares on him (Psalm 55:22). 1Peter 5:7 says "Give all your worries, anxieties and cares to God, for he cares about you." Remember you have the HolySpirit your senior partner who is always willing to help you and guide you through each day's problems (Romans 8:26, TLB).

That you should listen to the voice of the HolySpirit in everything you do and everywhere you go because only the Holyspirit can keep you on track and in line with God's will for your life.

Finally, don't assume that you know it all, always seek the help of the Holyspirit in all you do and also seek godly counsel from godly and people of great character that you can trust when you need it.

And as you obey this godly counsel from today's key verses, you can be rest assured that your body will glow with health, your very bones will vibrate with life and God will be pleased with you too because of your obedience to his word!

> **Remember, God's word is truth that brings life to every area of our lives, only if we obey!**

Do have a blessed and productive day!

DAY 29

FIX YOUR EYES ON GOD'S TRUTH

As you step out today, here's a reminder of God's word to you from Hebrews 12:2 [AMP] and Psalm 121:1-2.

> *"looking away from all that will distract us and] focusing our eyes on Jesus, who is the Author and Perfecter of faith [the first incentive for our belief and the One who brings our faith to maturity], who for the joy [of accomplishing the goal] set before Him endured the cross, disregarding the shame, and sat down at the right hand of the throne of God [revealing His deity, His authority, and the completion of His work]."*

Psalm 121:1-2 [AMP]
> *"I lift up my eyes to the mountains—*
>   *where does my help come from?*
> ^{2}*My help comes from the Lord,*
>   *the Maker of heaven and earth."*

The lyrics to the song 'Good Grace' by Hillsong is such a powerful reminder of God's word from today's key scriptures. Part of the lyrics of this song which I believe will strengthen your heart and faith this morning/today and as often as you listen to it is this –

" *So don't let your heart be troubled*

Hold your head up high
Don't fear no evil
Fix your eyes on this one truth
God is madly in love with you
So take courage
Hold on
Be strong
Remember where our help comes from"

So, no matter what the difficult situation or circumstances you might be going through right now is. Yes, it might be so painful that you ask God why? And you just might be in a state where you feel anxious and worried about all that is going on in your life right now. But my encouragement to you is – deliberately speak to your soul God's truth today.

Just like King David did in Psalm 42:5 when he was discouraged, disturbed and his soul was in turmoil *"**Why, my soul, are you downcast? Why so disturbed within me? Put your hope in God, for I will yet praise him, my Savior and my God"*** He spoke to his soul and told his soul to choose to hope in the Lord. He was intentionally about speaking and declaring to his soul and this is what you must also do, speak to your soul.

Apostle Paul also echoes these words in Romans 12:12 when he admonished the Christians in Rome to be 'joyful in hope'. This is never going to be easy but with the strength of the Holyspirit we are comforted and assured that the Lord is in the fire and the deepest waters with us.

His promise to us as his children is this *"**When you go through deep waters, I will be with you. When you go through rivers of difficulty, you will not drown. When you walk through the fire of*** *oppression, you will not be burned up; the flames will not consume you." – Isaiah 43:2*.

So, I encourage you as you listen to this song, to boldly declare God's truth over your situation. When you find yourself overwhelmed with your situation, plug in your ears, repeat again these lines and speak these words (God's truth) over your soul. Make it your declaration and confession and let your heart be captivated in the truth of these words knowing that God is madly in love with you.

Remember, you are more than a conqueror.

Do have a blessed and productive day!

DAY 30

CREATED TO DO GOOD WORKS

As you step out today, here's a reminder of God's word to you from Ephesians 2:10 [AMP].

> *¹⁰ "For we are His workmanship [His own masterwork, a work of art], created in Christ Jesus [reborn from above—spiritually transformed, renewed, ready to be used] for good works, which God prepared [for us] beforehand [taking paths which He set], so that we would walk in them [living the good life which He prearranged and made ready for us]."*

The [NIV] Translation says,

> *"For we are God's handiwork (workmanship) created in Christ Jesus to do good works, which God prepared in advance for us to do."*

The [NLT] translation says,

> *"For we are God's masterpiece. He has created us anew in Christ Jesus, so we can do the good things he planned for us long ago."*

Praise God! Today's bible verse reminds us of who we are in Christ. It emphasizes our Identity in Christ and it lays out for us the purpose for which we have been created – **To do Good Works**.

In a nutshell, today's scripture is simply your blueprint as a believer! It is your roadmap to living a life of impact, purpose, and influence. So, if you have sometimes, ever wondered what is the purpose of your life? Here it is -to do good works!

Good works are relative to every individual from offering your seat on a train or bus to providing food supplies to the less privileged. What is important is that you are constantly seeking opportunities to do good works, i.e. to put a smile on someone's face, to speaking an encouraging word to a broken heart and to simply just be a blessing to others without expecting anything in return.

Today's Bible verse echoes God's truth into our heart so that we can clearly focus and not be distracted by life frivolities. This means that we have to live each day with intentionality, making sure that everything we do is geared towards doing 'good works.' Doing Good works will involve different things to each of us as a believer, but the underlying principle is that you live life in such a way that your life brings beauty out of others and gives hope to them!

Jesus is our perfect example when it comes to doing good works. The bible says in Acts 10:38 that Jesus our Savior in whom we were created in his image and likeness also went about doing 'good' and used all that He had to bless others and to heal all those that were oppressed of the devil.

Therefore, as you go about your daily business and activities today, let this scripture rejuvenate your passion and desire to live a life dedicated to being a blessing to others. Let it also stir within you a renewed commitment that everything you do will be motivated by this one thing – to do good works. So, commit to using your gifts, talents, profession, skills, the unique abilities God has given to you to help your brother, sister neighbour, colleague, friend, family, business, church, partner, community, and nation etc. Don't wait to get a platform before you chose to do good works, start now from where you are.

Remember, don't do your good works for selfish gains, or to seek power or recognition or to impress or oppress others but instead use it to transform a life. Use it to bring hope, joy, and good news to others. Perhaps you feel unsure of what good works to embark on, I encourage you to start doing something with people around you. Also, ask the Holyspirit to show you want to do, He sure has loads of ideas to get you started.

Here's something to practice doing.

At the end of each day ask yourself the question, have I debited into my good works account today? and if the answer is no, don't beat yourself down but let it propel and spur you to make a commitment to do so another day the Lord will grace you to see.

Remember, when you do good works, you not only fulfil the very purpose for which God created you, but you can be sure that this will gladden the heart of the father and on judgment day, hear Him say to you "...Well done good and faithful son/daughter"- (Matthew 25:21).

Do have a blessed and productive day!

ABOUT BUSOLA ADUN

Busola Adun, fondly called MamaEagle, is an identity coach, an inspirational writer, speaker, song writer, worshipper, entrepreneur, and certified HR Consultant. She is a multifaceted woman with a passion for equipping and empowering people to understand and walk in the knowledge of their identity in order to live a victorious life Her evangelist ministry affords her the opportunity to share the good news of Christ with people of different cultures and faith and encourage believers to pursue their kingdom identity and be Christ influencers everywhere they go. She is the host of Identity Conference, Finding Hope in Community and founder of the Noble Woman Ministry, a ministry committed to inspiring hope and building faith in people through its activities and conferences. Especially empowering young people, particularly women, to understand and walk in the knowledge of their identity in Christ. She blogs at www.bzioninspires.com with a readership from over 135 countries. She inspires her readers with hope and faith found in God's living word to help them walk in their identity in Christ and live worthy of their call as ambassadors of Christ.

She and her husband, Femi Adun, through their mission ministry, Eagle World Outreach, serve and provide Apostolic leadership to churches in Europe, Africa, United States &

South America. They continue to impact believers across the body of Christ. Busola lives and thrives on Jesus, worship, fashion, and photography. Between writing her blog, honoring speaking engagements, leading a women's ministry, building her jewelry business, and running a productivity booster and HR consulting company with her husband She enjoys travelling with her husband and creating beautiful and precious memories with him, along with her three energetic, amazing, blessed, creative, and rapidly growing beautiful children, Joella, Israel, and Hadarah Adun.

Connect with Busola Adun
IG and Twitter: @bzionbabe
Facebook: Olubusola Adun